The Tie Protector

'Photographs by Anthony Dallas'

Integrity Finishes

Why it Matters

by

Kevin L. Smith

ISBN: 978-1-956884-40-1

Contributing Editor: All services completed by Imprint Productions, Inc.

Cover Design: All services completed by Imprint Productions, Inc.

Printed in the United States of America Published by Imprint Productions, Inc.

First Edition 2026

Award - 2024

Kevin Smith and Restoration Community Resources (RCR) were awarded the prestigious Non-Profit Organization of the Year IMPACT AWARD in 2024, presented by the City of South Fulton, Economic Development Office, Georgia.

The award honors local businesses and organizations for creating a significant positive community impact. The award was presented at the 2nd annual Impact Awards Dinner by the City of South Fulton, Georgia, on December 5, 2024.

Proclamation

City of South Fulton, Georgia
February 25, 2025

City of South Fulton, Georgia, recognizes Restoration Community Resources (RCR) Entrepreneurial Mentoring Program, established in 2004 by Minister Kevin L. Smith, whose vision is to successfully impact the lives of young men between the ages of 9 and 18 years through mentorship, with emphasis on education and exposure to entrepreneurial endeavors.

The mentorship of RCR offers a unique learning experience and plays a vital role in shaping young men to become entrepreneurs with the vision of becoming leaders in their families and the community.

The Proclamation was received for 20 years of dedicated service.

Foreword

In a world that prioritizes chaos, convenience, and the elevation of the personal 'brand,' one is fortunate to occasionally cross paths with a Kevin Smith. A husband, a father, a man of faith, an author, a businessman, an athlete, a mentor, and an entrepreneur, Kevin is that rare breed of individual who completes things. This means, simply put, that he can be relied upon not only to give you his word and commit to help, but also to invoke every resource at his disposal to see the task through.

He is a throwback – in the best sense of that word – to a different time that now seems ages ago, but which exists within our lifetime. It is only fitting that he is an authority to hold court on the topic of integrity.

This work could not be more timely, as it will prove to be a guidepost by which future generations can navigate the slings and arrows of a most challenging time in our history. We need to hear from Kevin Smith about integrity.

The dictionary defines *integrity* this way:

- The quality of being honest and having strong moral principles; moral uprightness
- The state of being whole and undivided
- The condition of being unified, unimpaired, or sound in construction
- Internal consistency or lack of corruption

Those who have been fortunate enough to engage with Kevin Smith have perceived all of the above – and more – in the unwavering consistency and the principled approach by which he lives his life. Integrity Finishes is merely an outward expression of standards and values that live in full force on the inside, from a man who has walked the talk for decades. There is no person I know who is more qualified to address this vital topic than my longtime friend and co-conspirator. He is indeed the embodiment of integrity in our community.

I have known Kevin for decades, and while I consider him a close friend and a valued member of my inner circle, I respect him and honor his strong example even more. Among our many connections, we have attended the same house of worship for more than 20 years and have served together on the ministry leadership team there.

One of the coolest characteristics Kevin displays is the fact that he has no perceptible moods…there are no swings of emotion, anger, or volatility. He is smooth, quiet. , and consistent. Always on hand but never the center of attention, Kevin prefers to do, rather than talk, and often moves in silence to bless the lives of others in profound ways. The most admirable trait of a man of faith is not thunderous preaching or melodious singing or even profound twists of linguistic artistry, but rather the willingness to put the needs of others ahead of his own. That Christlike sense of selflessness is among Kevin's most admirable traits.

Kevin Smith is a man who lives to serve. He has run a prison outreach that turned lives around and gave men purpose both during and after incarceration, supporting the complicated process of becoming a better man and reintegrating into society afterwards.

Kevin teaches integrity. He has led one of the area's longest tenured and most successful youth mentorship programs, taking on the entire spectrum of behaviors, moods, and attitudes that often impede young people's progress. Kevin and his team have impacted thousands of lives – not only the young men themselves but their mothers, fathers, siblings, peers. , and future spouses – while coaching, nurturing, and assisting emerging leaders in search of their purpose and calling.

Kevin imparts integrity. He has demonstrated discipline and dedication in ministry, lending his talents to whatever task he might be assigned, from preaching bible study and leading our men's ministry to counseling, baptism, weddings. , and homegoing services.

Kevin exemplifies integrity. The man is equipped with the whole tool kit and has blessed our world through the application of his many gifts. Kevin exemplifies the meaning of integrity in the way he serves the community. He has kept his office in a somewhat disadvantaged community, resisting the temptation to flee to the suburbs as have so many organizations. He is a leader of the business association that seeks to support and sustain the economic viability of that corridor, lending his full support to cleanup drives, fundraising events, food giveaways, back-to-school events, community medical screenings, and countless grand openings and other positive endeavors.

And perhaps his most remarkable service to our community is to have partnered with his beautiful wife Myrtice in the raising of an incredible young adult son who is blazing trails of his own in his father's footsteps. There is no greater contribution one can make to society than to ensure that his children are solid citizens who love God, work hard, care about others, and walk in integrity themselves.

It is clear that this man, Kevin Smith, is cut from peculiar cloth. While his life might appear spectacular to some, and some of his accomplishments unachievable for most, the conclusion of the matter is that he walks in integrity, which brings us back to this dynamic work.

Read it, share it, teach it to your kids, and read it again. The book, like its author, is an agent of change that we need in these perilous times. Bravo, Brother Kevin, and thank you for allowing me to travel with you on part of your journey. Integrity Finishes, folks…now what are you prepared to do?

Lonnie Viccarro "Vic" Bolton
Communications Consultant and Long-Time Friend

Integrity Finishes

Why it Matters

Preface

I have cared about success for people for as long as can remember, and I want to share some lessons on what I have learned as an entrepreneur with more than 25 years of experience and as a mentor to people from all walks of life.

As our lives and world continue to change, it is my belief that integrity will be the consistent component to finishing what we set out to do.

As you read this book,
you will ask yourself this question, :
"Am I a person of integrity?"

Integrity Finishes explains, with example after example, the importance of being productive in your life. When we go through life with integrity, our words and actions line up with each other. Integrity Finishes guides us to finish (complete) the assignment, task, or promise.

I remember a time when a person would give their word to complete a task, an assignment, or give a promise of completion. There was no further discussion. It was just assumed that the person would follow through and complete the task or assignment. In short, they would complete what they promised.

To me, the words we speak to others are very important. The words we speak do affect others. It is very important that we honor the words we speak. We honor the words with our actions. As it relates to integrity, actions actually speak louder than words.

I desire the reader of this book to be encouraged and challenged to complete their goals in life.

As we go through life, we are going to experience disappointments because that is part of living, and no one is exempt from them. We can also learn from our disappointments; they help us prepare for our next assignment or opportunity.

We are winners when we do not allow disappointments to paralyze us. We cannot change the past, but we can do something to change the future.

The demonstration of integrity in life is important, because our actions speak louder than our words.

As a young man, there was a statement that stood out to me. As I became an adult, I learned more about it. "Sticks and stones may break my bones, but words will never hurt me." As I became an adult, I came to realize the statement was not true. I learned that words are very important because they can encourage or discourage. Decide today to be an encourager to others.

Many people have great ideas, but they stop before they get started. Often, when we get an idea, our friends or family members may not see what we see, and they might not encourage us.

Their discouragement of your idea does not mean that you should not pursue your idea or invention. Dreams should be pursued; just remember that not everyone will endorse your dream.

But remember this: Just because you do not get an endorsement from someone else does not mean you should stop pursuing your ideas and dreams.

As the reader of Integrity Finishes, you will realize that there is a distinct difference between integrity and "good intentions."

Integrity will: Exemplify a positive example, not just when the situation is convenient. Build trust and confidence with your families, friends, teammates, business partners, and co-workers.

A person of integrity will honor their word and follow through on what was promised. On the other hand, a person of good intentions will have a plan with no execution or completion date. Intentions remain incomplete because there is not a designed plan of action. When people do not have a plan of action, they often fail to complete the goal.

You can have a plan of action, but it is key that you put forth action with your plan.

There must be actions to match your plan, or it is not a plan of action. A plan without action will not be completed. Character separates the person of integrity from the person with intentions.

This is the reason for the book Integrity Finishes. I believe you will finish!

Keep growing.

Kevin L. Smith
Atlanta, Georgia
Date, 2025

TABLE OF CONTENTS

Kevin Smith's Integrity Terms of Understanding

Integrity is developed and not inherited.

Integrity causes you to do what is right when no one is watching.

People are not born with integrity; it is a decision you make every day.

Integrity defines your words and your actions as one.

Integrity honors commitments, regardless of the disappointments.
The person who quits can never win.

Integrity has a voice; it is your actions.

Integrity does not try. Try is an attempt that will always fail. Have you ever "tried" to sit in a chair? You do not try; you just sit in the chair.

Integrity is not determined by your position, title, or income. Integrity is based on the decisions you execute.

Integrity is identified not by how others treat you, but by how you treat others.

A person of integrity is a winner.

About the Author

Kevin L. Smith is a businessman and visionary leader who devotes his expertise to entrepreneur mentoring, training, and developing people. His insight on the necessity of maintaining integrity throughout his life is a true testimony of encouragement and empowerment.

In 1985, Kevin relocated to Atlanta, Georgia from Philadelphia, Pennsylvania, as an executive recruiter with Execu Search, Inc. His responsibility was to assist in opening the company's first franchise office.

The success of the Atlanta office under his leadership earned notable mentions in the Atlanta Journal Constitution and Black Enterprise magazine.

Kevin is the inventor of the Smithi Tie Protector, which received a Design Patent and Trademark. The Smithi Tie Protector is currently being sold online.

Kevin is the CEO of Restoration Community Resources, Inc., which is a 501(c)3 nonprofit organization that offers an Entrepreneurial Mentoring program that is designed to assist young men with recognizing and fulfilling their purpose in life.

Kevin has been married to Myrtice Smith for 37 years, and the couple has a son, Kennington Lloyd Smith III. Kevin is an ordained Minister at World Changers Church International in College Park, Georgia.

Kevin graduated from Lincoln University in Pennsylvania with a Bachelor of Arts in Finance. He was initiated into Omega Psi Phi Fraternity at Lincoln University, and he is currently a member of the Zeta Mu Nu chapter in Georgia.

Dedication

I dedicate this book to my wife, Myrtice Y. Smith; our son, Kennington Lloyd Smith III; my parents, Mildred A. Smith and Kennington Lloyd Smith, Jr., both deceased; and my mother-in-law, Opal Lee.

Acknowledgements

I am fortunate to have important people in my life who have given me inspiration and life lessons. Here is a partial list of these people.

Dr. Creflo A. Dollar, Jr, Spiritual Father

Minister Tommie Garner, Jr, and Brent Williams, co-founders of Restoration Community Resources

Past and Current Mentors of Restoration Community Resources

Alumni and Current Young Entrepreneurs of Restoration Community Resources

Parents of Alumni and Current Young Entrepreneurs of Restoration Community Resources

Past and Present Board Members of Restoration Community Resources

Pillars of the Aftercare Program Discipleship House

World Changers Church International Prison Ministry

Voices of Deliverance Prayer Team

Past and Present Board Members of Old National Merchants Association

Minister Jimmie L. Lucas, Jr., for assisting with my first manuscript

Mallory Sanford and Leroy Franklin (deceased), co-founders of Execu Search

Imprint Productions, Inc. and Henry E. Liebling for the completion of this book

Walter A. Rodgers, Intellect Property Law

What Do People Say About Integrity?

When you think of the word integrity, what comes to your mind?

"Integrity" is defined by the Webster dictionary as soundness, undivided, honesty, and unity.

As a mentor and workshop leader, I have witnessed integrity from many people who represented different life experiences, including various ages, genders, professions, and backgrounds high school, to college. I am grateful to have worked with such diverse people.

What does integrity look like to you?

- Honesty
- Place of comfort
- Truth
- Person of their word
- Consistency
- Concerned about others
- Demonstrated by taking action and not just speaking words
- A rare quality
- Making the right decision when no one is watching
- Pride in who you represent
- Character is what keeps you in the position you were placed
- Honoring your word
- It's an example to learn from
- Dependable

I have also asked this related question:

> **What is your definition of a person who *__does not__* operate with integrity?**
>
> **What does that look like to you?**

Here are some of the responses I have heard:

- No commitment
- Not dependable
- A person who is not a team player
- A person who does not follow through on their word

-

> "People with integrity expect to be believed, if not, they let time prove them right."
>
> *~Ann Landers, American Columnist*

What does integrity mean to you?

____

____

____

____

CHAPTER ONE

Your Journey is Just as Important as the Destination

Finishing what you start is a vital part of life. Stay at it.

My message throughout this book is to "stay at it" and finish. Remember, you cannot accomplish your goals if you do not finish them.

Starting is important. Finishing is just as important.

Are you familiar with New Year's resolutions? When we make a New Year's resolution, we are communicating about wanting to make a change in our lives. We are saying the words and committing to a goal. A person's New Year's resolution could be about losing weight, saving money, purchasing a new home, or finishing an academic degree. The question is: How many people who make New Year's resolutions complete what they started? It depends on their commitment.

Change is challenging because it removes routine from our lives.

I think of a routine as all those things performed regularly.

The reason many people do not complete (or achieve) their resolutions is because they are too comfortable in their routine.

In order for us to grow and move toward achieving our goals, we need to move past what is comfortable.

A plan of action and completion of the plan are as important as starting.

We need to take action and follow-up and follow through. Our plan of action keeps us focused when procrastination and discouragement attempt to derail us. When we have a plan of action, we know the path to follow.

Your plan of action and your vision work together like a compass to keep you focused when obstacles come into your path.

We need to write down our action plan, which will lead us to completion.

When we get discouraged or disappointed, we can go back to our written plan to help get refocused on what we need so that we can move forward. Without having a written plan of action, we can let our disappointments lead us back to being comfortable. If we are "too comfortable," we are probably not moving forward with the actions needed to complete our goal.

We must see ourselves succeeding.

We must not stay locked in our comfort zone. When we remain the same, we are not changing.

The closer we get to our goal, the more challenges we face. As we overcome these challenges, we are completing the steps in our plan of action, which is finishing, (completing, and achieving) our goal.

"When we fail to plan, we plan to fail."

We cannot follow a plan if that plan does not exist.

Some goals may take longer to accomplish.

If you decide to complete a college degree part-time while you are working a full-time job, it will take longer to accomplish than if you were a full-time student.

The key is to stay focused on the goals that you start, regardless of how long it may take to complete.

I have friends who have taken the bar exam to become lawyers and others who have taken the exam to become Certified Public Accountants (CPA). Some of these friends have passed the exams the first time. Others have taken the test multiple times before passing.

Their common goal for success was that they did not quit.

It's about finishing the goal, not how long it may take.

Success

What does success look like to you?

The Integrity Journey

A journey is to advance from one place to another. The destination is the place of completion or end of that particular journey.

The journey is a process.

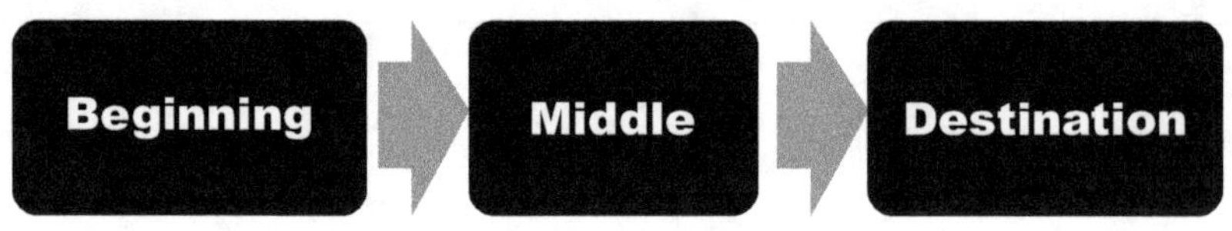

There are planned journeys in life that we initiate.

The journey begins: What do I want to accomplish?

I make a decision that I want to lose weight and start eating healthy. I begin with my plan of action. For example, I put into my plan of action a scheduled time to exercise each day. In my plan of action, I identify foods and snacks I need to eliminate.

I put in my action plan that I do not eat past a certain time in the evening.

The action plan will be challenging because it is a change in my routine. My ability to execute my action plan impacts my ability to reach my destination.

The Beginning

Some journeys are not planned.

We are living our lives and we can go on an unexpected journey.

I had just graduated from college and received my first job offer as an actuary with John Hancock Insurance in Boston, Massachusetts. I was visiting some friends to discuss my relocation and new position.

After I left my friend's home, I got into a head-on collision in my father's car, and the car was totaled. I remember lying in the ambulance. All kinds of thoughts were going through my mind. As the ambulance arrived at the hospital, I remembered being rushed to the emergency room. The next thing I remembered was opening my eyes and seeing my mother and father.

The doctor entered the room and explained I was fortunate to be alive. He also explained my schedule for physical therapy, and hopefully, my leg would not have to be amputated. The glass from the windshield went into my face, and if it was one inch higher, a piece of glass would have gone into my eye, and I could have been blinded in my left eye.

The following Monday, I contacted John Hancock Insurance Company and informed them of my accident. Due to my injuries, the job offer was rescinded.

Months later, I fully recovered to continue the journey I had not planned. I was thankful to recover at my parents' home.

What did I want to accomplish?

My plan of action: Find a position that could offer opportunity, advancement, and support for my life. I was moving forward regardless of the previous events that had taken place. My mind-set was to be thankful I was alive and continue with my action plan to secure the position I desired.

Continuing with my job search, I received a position with the State of New Jersey Department of Community Affairs. I was a Field Auditor in the energy conservation unit. Two years later, I accepted a position with a consulting firm based in Washington, D.C. However, I was to work in Philadelphia, Pennsylvania. Unexpectedly, and after two years, I was laid off from that job.

Then I was going on another unplanned journey.

I was back in on the job market. Continuing in my job search, I was offered a position in Philadelphia, with the Southeastern Pennsylvania Transportation Authority (SEPTA).

With each of these career opportunities, I was being prepared for my next journey to relocate to Atlanta, Georgia. My consistency of purpose was a key element in continuing my journey.

The Middle

A plan of action is a crucial guide that propels you to the destination.

You must put something in writing to stay focused on your plan. As you go through your journey to reach your destination, you will change certain habits and make adjustments in your life.

On our journey to our destination, we experience disappointments. I ask you not to allow the disappointments to discourage you. We should view our disappointments as an opportunity to improve. We can choose to embrace these challenges as part of the journey.

Do not be intimidated by these challenges; learn from them.

Here's something interesting to remember about people. As we tackle and overcome disappointments and challenges, we gain confidence in our ability to keep moving forward to reach our destination. It helps build our resilience.

The Destination

The task or goal has been reached.

It is important to be thankful for your accomplishment.

I also encourage you to reflect on the journey that got you to this accomplishment. Consider some of the lessons you learned and any disappointments you were able to overcome. These are considered important life lessons that build your character and integrity.

What did you learn on this journey that will help you reach other destinations?

You may not understand everything about your journey until you reach your destination.

This is the reason why the journey is just as important as the destination.

Perseverance

The dictionary definition of perseverance is steady persistence in a course of action, especially, in light of difficulties, obstacles, or discouragement.

How you view challenges will determine how you advance on your journey to your destination.

While on your journey to your destination or goal, remember that challenges are meant to be overcome. They are learning experiences.

When you look at a glass of water, do you look at it as half-full or half-empty? It is your mindset that determines if the glass is half-full or half-empty.

When you are on your journey, there are things that will happen that you may not understand. You may say to yourself, "Why is this happening?" and "Why is this happening to me?"

When you "see yourself" at the destination, it helps build your perseverance and motivation.

Chapter Review: Stop, Start, Continue, and Finish

Writing this book is a living example of Stop, Start, Continue, and Finish.

My hope is that this section provides encouragement and helpful tips to you.

Stop

When we stop, it signals there is no movement, you have a decision to make.

Let's look at some of your options.

- You can decide to move forward.
- You can decide to remain in the stop position.
- You can decide to turn around and go in another direction.

I came to a stop in the process of this book.
- Should I continue to write this book?
- Why should I continue to write this book?

There are times in life when people stop themselves…before they even start.

____

____

____

____

Start

I want you to remember that you cannot complete a goal (reach your destination) until you start. If you have stopped, now might be the time to start again.

After you start the process of moving toward your goal, the challenge is to keep your focus.

Understand your "why"

What is your "why"? What are your reasons for completing the assignment or goal. ?

You will encounter obstacles along the way, and you will have disappointments. Please remember, this is part of the process.

Allow the obstacles and disappointments to strengthen you to continue with your goals.

Knowing your "why" is a reminder to you of the importance of completing the goal.

____

____

____

____

Continue

When we are in the continue stage, our commitment is enhanced by the encouragements we have received and obstacles we have overcome.

What is commitment?

Commitment is focusing on the promises we have made, regardless of the tests we encounter along our journey.

As we continue our journey, we ask ourselves, "What will it take on my part to complete this goal?"

____

____

____

____

Finish

When you finish achieving your goal, it will give you confidence to complete future goals. In addition, it will allow you to encourage others to complete their goals.

Chapter Take-Aways

Please write down several points you want to remember and apply from this chapter.

CHAPTER TWO

Integrity, Challenges, and Investments

My Comfort Zone.

I decided to leave my job in Philadelphia to relocate to Atlanta and become a recruiter with Execu Search's first franchise office. Introduced to this opportunity by Van Corbin.

This move was totally out of my comfort zone.

I want to say that when you are out of your comfort zone, it is not necessarily bad, it is merely a recognition that you are making a change (or taking a growth step) from what is familiar to you.

I was leaving a corporate job with a regular salary and benefits to begin a 100% commission position. In addition, I would be entirely responsible for my relocation expenses.

You can only imagine the conversations I was having with family members and friends about relocating to Atlanta with no defined wages and benefits. I remember that "everyone" had an opinion.

.

Staying Focused.

It was important for me to stay focused on the goals I wanted to accomplish.

I dismissed the thought of failure and concentrated on becoming an intricate part of the Execu Search organization.

Learning the recruiting business.

I discovered the industry was super competitive. Many Fortune 500 companies were using recruiting firms, and most of these firms had established relationships with recruiters. My job was to identify companies that were open to starting new relationships.

I had many conversations with these companies. Unfortunately, the conversations were very short in length, and they would often end abruptly. I maintained a positive attitude even though I was told: "No, not at this time" or "No, we are not interested." My attitude was part of my preparation to stay committed to my decision to be successful in the recruiting industry.

My disappointments became my motivation.

I was pleasant and positive while making the calls day after day, regardless of the responses I was receiving. This paid off.

I finally received an opportunity to work with a company to recruit pharmaceutical representatives. I was prepared when the opportunity presented itself. I presented qualified candidates to the client company; and the company was impressed and hired several candidates I presented.

As a result of hiring these individuals, the company gained confidence in my ability to effectively meet their goals. This led me to additional assignments from the company.

Now, with documented successes, I was able to establish successful relationships with other major pharmaceutical companies. My perseverance led to success with many clients.

I learned an important lesson.

When preparation meets opportunity, success can follow.

New Business Venture

After a few years with Execu Search, a co-worker, Lance Coachman, and I decided to form a partnership named Excel Executive Recruiters. It was a tough decision to leave Execu Search. At the time, I believed it was the best decision for my family and me.

Integrity Investments

As you continue to read this chapter, remember the importance of making integrity investments. When we make an integrity investment, we plant seeds that grow.

My role in the partnership was to utilize my recruiting skills in the pharmaceutical and biotechnology industries. Lance was focused on the financial and accounting industries. A few other recruiters joined our firm.

We continued to make a positive impact in the recruiting industry and established a portfolio of client companies. Excel Executive Recruiters became known for professionalism and dependability.

After several years with the firm, I was approached with an opportunity to work with a startup pharmaceutical company. The assignment was to assist in the expansion of a National Sales Division. I met with Lance and informed him of the opportunity. I was not seeking to leave the partnership; the firm was doing well, and Lance was not only a business partner, he was a friend.

However, the opportunity with the startup pharmaceutical company would not allow me to continue as a partner. Lance and I decided he would retain full ownership. As my partnership with the firm was terminated, I exceeded my financial commitments. This was an integrity investment.

The opportunity with Astra Pharmaceutical company was a successful transition. I was able to develop excellent relationships with the management team and was asked to participate in a second expansion of their national sales team.

I contacted Mallory Sanford and Leroy Franklin and arranged to meet them in Philadelphia at the Execu Search Headquarters. During the meeting I was given the opportunity to explain my initial departure and apologize. Additionally, I was able to explain the reason I wanted to partner with Execu Search on the expansion with Astra Pharmaceuticals. Mallory and Leroy stated they would review the proposal and contact me to schedule a follow-up meeting to further discuss the details. During our follow-up meeting, Mallory and Leroy offered me the option to acquire the Execu Search Atlanta franchise office. Thankful, grateful, and excited, I returned to Atlanta.

Establishing the Execu Search Atlanta Franchise Office

My first hire was Alexis Jackson. Thank you, Alexis! She believed in me when all we had was a vision. Alexis and I communicated the values and standards of a successful office environment. We knew the type of team we wanted to assemble. It was simple: We would operate our office with integrity and excellence. Felicia Freeman was the next person I hired, who ultimately became my business partner in the Atlanta office. We were committed to maintaining the integrity standard throughout our office.

Within several years, Execu Search had six franchise offices throughout the country. The Atlanta office had become one of their most successful franchises. We were able to successfully assist entry-level people in starting a career with pharmaceutical and biotech companies. In addition, we assisted experienced people in advancing their careers in these industries. Some of our accounts included Johnson & Johnson, Ortho Biotech, Kimberly Clark Surgical Division, AstraZeneca, Genentech, and Amgen.

Integrity Investments bring you future benefits

When we make a financial investment, our goal is to increase our money (our wealth), over time. When we make a time investment in a specific project or goal, we expect the investment to pay off in the future.

When we make an integrity investment today, it builds trust, strengthens our relationships, and creates a foundation for long-term success.

The skills I acquired during my years in the recruiting industry were invaluable, such as interviewing, contract negotiation, networking, and public speaking.
I have been able to use these skills later in my career and life to expand the entrepreneurial mentoring program.

Remember, you can make integrity investments in every area of life.

Examples of Integrity Investments

Example #1

While working alongside a vice president of software engineering, a colleague came forward with serious accusations against my supervisor concerning inappropriate behavior. When this colleague confided in me about their experience, I felt compelled to delve deeper, and their unsettling responses raised significant concerns for me. Subsequently, I found myself in a position where HR and my supervisor's superior sought my perspective on the allegations.
I made a firm decision to remain truthful and stand by my supervisor, as I believed in the importance of integrity. I carefully recounted my observations about my supervisor's conduct while also addressing my colleague's peculiar and inappropriate behavior, including their choice of a vulgar Wi-Fi name on their phone. In that pivotal moment, I prioritized honesty over comfort, recognizing the lasting value of integrity.

Years later, my own work ethic faced scrutiny, but thanks to my unwavering commitment to doing the right thing, my organization stood firmly by my side.

Example #2

I remember being laid off from my first job after only two years of work, fresh out of grad school. I had been desperately searching for a job for over eight months when I heard about a position in a school district (in another state) that was four hours away. To have an interview for the job, I would need to travel those four hours.

To my surprise, the individual I met never interviewed me for the position. We talked for almost three hours about almost everything EXCEPT the position. He even took me around and introduced me to the other staff members before mentioning anything about the position.

I was surprised when he told me the job was mine if I wanted it. I asked him about the interview, and he said, "I have been interviewing you for the last two hours." He also said, "I have a good feeling about you, and I would love to have you join the team." The fact that he was willing to take such a chance on me, a person he had never met before, made a lasting impression on me and impressed upon my heart with the importance of giving a person a chance. I accepted the job.

Fast forward many years, and the gentleman who had hired me had retired; now I was the Director of Social Work Services for a school district. It was the department's custom to partner with local universities to allow interns to shadow within our department. One particular year, I received a phone call from a young lady who wanted to intern with us, but her school was in another state. Ordinarily, I wouldn't even consider such a request because I would have to travel to that state (which was two hours away), to attend a field placement orientation.

I had every logical reason not to do it, but I thought back to many years previously when my former supervisor gave this out-of-state kid a shot without even knowing me. At that moment, I decided to make an "integrity investment" and provide an opportunity to another person, just like I had been provided early in my career. Needless to say, the intern worked out great and even got a full-time position after completing her internship.

But that's not the end of the story. Many years later, I left the position I held and found myself in search of another job. This time, I had a wife and son, and things were starting to become really stressful. I applied for position after position with no luck. Then one day, I called the intern I had once supervised and told her about my predicament. She never forgot the grace I extended to her in getting the internship and even the salaried position in our former school district. She was now in a new school district, the one I was applying to work in, but I couldn't make any headway. To make a long story short, she helped me navigate the process and played an instrumental role in helping me secure my current position. Needless to say, the "integrity investment" I made in her many years ago paid off for me at a time when I needed it most.

Testimonials

Herman Cortez

"I have known Kevin Smith slightly over 20 years. This has been during my tenure in the pharmaceutical / and biotech industry in his capacity as a recruiter for Execu Search. Kevin's strengths are many. Most obvious is his amazing capacity to connect with his clients, unbelievable work ethic, and his listening / and communication skills. I was fortunate to have his talents available to me on many occasions during recruitment efforts. Kevin successfully placed me as a Director of Field Training in the Pharmaceutical industry. He is an extremely experienced individual who delivers on his promises. Kevin, it has been an honor to work with you, my friend."

Leon Robinson

"I have known Kevin Smith since high school. After college, Kevin and I had the opportunity to work in a professional capacity for the State of New Jersey. After completing my MBA and working for several years, Kevin and I reconnected, and he informed me he had relocated to Atlanta with Execu Search. I was confident he would be successful because of his character and work ethic."

"I was in the Insurance industry when Kevin approached me with a new opportunity in the pharmaceutical industry. I understood the importance of networking and maintaining relationships in one's career. I trusted Kevin and interviewed for the position and received my first position in the pharmaceutical industry with Astra Pharmaceuticals. After a number of years with Astra, Kevin told me about another upward opportunity, this time with Ortho Biotech, that would take me back to New Jersey. The timing was right and was a great decision for my family. I recently retired from Ortho Biotech after 25 years.

Kevin has made a major impact nationally in the pharmaceutical industry with the placement of diversity talent."

Eric Gibbs

"When I think of Kevin Smith, the following quote comes to mind. 'Success is a journey, not a destination.' These words ring true as I describe the role Kevin played in my life. He has been a role model, mentor, advisor, brother in Christ, but most importantly, he Is someone I am proud to call my friend."

"My relationship with Kevin started over 20 years ago when I got a call from his recruiting agency about a job with an up-and-coming biotech company called Amgen. At 26 years of age, I was gainfully employed with the world's largest pharmaceutical company, Pfizer Pharmaceutical. I had just been promoted, and I had recently completed my MBA at Johns Hopkins University. I had no intention of going to work for a biotech company because my future with Pfizer seemed very bright and promising."

"During my initial call with Kevin, something happened, and a divine connection was formed. Consequently, Kevin convinced me to at least interview for the position with Amgen."

"Prior to the interview, we prayed about the position, which was unique in a professional setting. The interview went well, I got an offer, and I accepted the position with Amgen. Fortunately, Amgen experienced massive growth while other companies in the pharmaceutical industry saw tremendous cutbacks."

"Not only was I blessed to be able to grow my career at Amgen, I was able to develop different skills that have afforded me opportunities above what I would have ever thought, dreamed, or imagined."

"I have been blessed to advance my career to Senior Executive within the Biotech Industry."

"I know now Kevin was placed in my life by God, and I am so thankful for his wisdom and encouragement."

Stephanie Fennell
(Former Sales Training Manager, Ortho Biotech)

"I had the pleasure of meeting Kevin Smith in 1992. I was living outside of Washington, D.C., and working for the Xerox Corporation. This was my first "real job," and I was not seeing it as a career, but was also not actively looking to change occupations. Looking back, it must have been divine intervention that brought Kevin Smith into my life.

Kevin owned an executive recruiting firm. He contacted me and asked if I would be interested in looking at another career opportunity. I asked what the position entailed; he stated it was with a pharmaceutical company named Ciba-Geigy. A company I had never heard of. He suggested I listen to the opportunity and let him know my impression of the company. He scheduled the interview; the interview went very well, and I was offered a position with Ciba-Geigy as a Sales Representative. The position allowed me to gain invaluable experience in the pharmaceutical industry, which prepared me for future opportunities.

In addition, Kevin became a trusted recruiter for me. He was well respected in the pharmaceutical recruiting industry by his colleagues, executives in the industry, and the Association of Pharmaceutical Representatives.

The professional presentation and integrity demonstrated to me by Kevin resulted in me referring other talented people to him; these were people who I knew were looking for better opportunities.

After a corporate downsizing and buyout. I moved so that I could work for the Pepsi Corporation. This position was not a good fit for me. Kevin seemed to have perfect timing; he contacted me with a great opportunity with Ortho Biotech, a Johnson & Johnson company. I interviewed for the position and was offered a job as a product specialist. I successfully worked at Johnson & Johnson for 13 years and was promoted to numerous positions. Kevin was a primary recruiter for the Johnson & Johnson organization because he consistently supplied talented individuals who were making an impact in the organization.

Kevin is a man of integrity and character who goes beyond his profession; he has always been encouraging and uplifting. As an entrepreneur and man of faith, he is a much-needed role model for others."

Brian K. Lewis
(Former Vice President of Diversity, Kimberly-Clark Corporation)

"I have known Kevin Smith for over 20 years. During that time, Kevin has been a constant and consistently positive influence in my life. Kevin has been a friend, minister, mentor, and role model for me."

"First and most importantly, Kevin possesses and demonstrates integrity. This goes well beyond doing what he says he will do. His commitment was consistent and strong. In the fifteen years of doing business with Kevin, he has never missed a deadline, never fallen short of expectations, and never failed to follow up."

"He has provided wisdom and guidance to me in professional and spiritual matters. He has served as my representative in both areas by presenting expert instruction to teams under my guidance. He never fell short of expectations."

"In short, Kevin is an A-lister that I have not, and would not, hesitate to give my highest recommendation."

Julius B. Dixon
(Former Regional Business Director, Pharmaceutical Industry)

"Default integrity and honesty are essential in professional and personal relationships and the foundation in building a trusting relationship."

"I first met Kevin approximately twenty-one years ago. He was the owner of an Execu Search, Inc. office, an executive search firm. Execu Search was hired by my former employer to support a national sales force expansion. Kevin's firm was specifically hired to assist us in adding diverse personnel to our expansion efforts. At the end of the assignment, Kevin and the Execu Search company received exceptional reviews from our company.

The talent Kevin provided to us during our national expansion significantly contributed to our success as an organization during the subsequent years. As a result of Kevin's professionalism, integrity, and the services he provided, we established a trusted business relationship through my years with the organization."

"Kevin and I have maintained a personal relationship over the years. I value our relationship and friendship. When I think of Kevin, I know he is a role model of our fraternity's cardinal principles of manhood, scholarship, perseverance, and uplift. I am honored to call him my friend and brother in Christ."

Deborah Jones King
(Former Regional Business Director, Roche Pharmaceuticals)

"Kevin Smith is the epitome of a Godly, professional gentleman. During my search for pharmaceutical representatives, he was attentive to details and always responsive. Kevin understood that only his best candidates would be considered and never gave me less. We never discussed the importance of integrity;however, he operated with that implied knowledge at every level. Kevin not only supplied me with excellent candidates, but he coached and mentored these candidates, so that they could reach their full earning potential."

"The candidates took on the professional aura of Kevin; his gentle manner was seasoned with a humble confidence to succeed. Kevin never displayed impatience but was always ready to listen to his client's needs and requirements, while balancing his desire to successfully place each candidate."

"Kevin also understood the pharmaceutical industry standards, and he never presented candidates with questionable credentials or marred backgrounds. He knew his trade well and recruited candidates who were not only excellent on paper, but they proved to be exceptional employees with potential for promotion. I always enjoyed working with Kevin because he made my job of bringing diversity to my company easy and allowed me to have an immense sense of pride in presenting his very strong candidates to my organization."

Donna Vaughn
(Former District Manager, Genentech, Inc.)

"I had my choice of a number of recruiters as I prepared to launch a new sales team. Kevin Smith was the answer to a manager's prayer when you are faced with building a sales team from the ground up."

"He raised the bar for all recruiters who came after him in my professional arena. Some recruiters were only interested in earning the commission if you hired one of their candidates. Kevin was interested in screening the candidate that you could hire, retain, and develop."

"In my industry, Biotechnology, the ability to hire top talent that could be developed for the future was just as important as the person who could deliver sales today. Kevin's integrity played a great role in his decisions to move a candidate forward. He took the time with the candidate to ensure that he was not sending me some other manager's problem. Many of the candidates that I received from his firm went to other roles within our organization. Those who chose to be career salespeople proved to be consistent high performers. In short, when I received a candidate from him, I knew that I was getting top talent."

"He was a great listener, and that boded well for his ability to match me with candidates that I would connect with. I sincerely believe when a person has integrity as a value, they perform with excellence. That would represent Kevin. He definitely had insight to read people and would send me the best person for my organization. That is a very high standard from a person with integrity."

Felicia Freeman
(Former Partner at Execu Search)

"I have known many professionals through my career in marketing and sales. Upon meeting Kevin Smith, I was able to experience a true man of honor and integrity. Kevin gave me an opportunity to work for Execu Search in 1998. I had no experience in the recruiting industry, but he saw something I could not see in myself. A franchise owner who has the ability to propel the staff into greatness is to be commended. Kevin displayed integrity every day with Execu Search. He was consistent, never made excuses, and always put the staff first before himself. There were days that I felt uneasy due to my lack of knowledge and experience in the recruiting industry, but I was encouraged and reassured by Kevin."

"He mentored me by taking time to demonstrate what an excellent recruiter should exemplify in every area. If there was a need in the office, Kevin made certain the need was taken care of immediately with no delay. I was equipped with the necessary tools to gain a strong reputation in the pharmaceutical industry. Kevin would not compromise the business in any capacity. Opportunities were presented to Execu Search that would have been of great financial benefit to the organization, but when not of integrity, they were not pursued."

"As an owner, Kevin refused to put selfish motives above integrity; I definitely admired that quality. The best mentor is one who teaches without knowing they are teaching a lesson or principle. Kevin took me under his wing without reservation. The wing Kevin extended to me gave me courage and strength to operate in excellence, personally and professionally. Thank you, Kevin, you never made me feel like a follower but a leader in the making."

Alexis Jackson

"Sometimes, we come across a person who knows what his purpose in life is. While most of us are trying to figure out dinner, this purposeful individual created a manageable path for others to follow. This is Kevin Smith. I have known Kevin since 1994. When he started his Execu Search franchise office in Atlanta, I was his first hire. He led the company with integrity, which was the foundation that helped usher in its success. Others were hired as the office continued to grow; the integrity mantra held our office together throughout the industry. He knows why he was put on earth: to help others find their way. He is a mentor, business leader, devout family man, inventor, and Minister who enjoys seeing people succeed.

His mentoring program helps young men discover and shape their potential for a successful future. He provides insight, finances, and examples of integrity. The mentors who assist Kevin in the program do an excellent job of demonstrating the challenging obstacles that happen in life situations and how they can be better prepared to succeed. Several of the young entrepreneurs in the mentoring program have moved on to become successful business owners and leaders throughout the nation.

The business leadership he displayed is evident in that his purpose is being fulfilled throughout the community, where he is well-known and respected. He's the man who has tentacles that reach far and wide into successful areas.

Kevin is one of a kind. His gentle demeanor makes him approachable and easy to engage in conversation. As you read this book, you will feel his spirit and see for yourself what a special person he is to our generation."

Mallory Sanford
(Founder of Executive Search, Inc.)

"I have known Kevin Smith for thirty-five years. When I think of the definition of integrity, I think of Kevin. I had the pleasure of hiring Kevin in 1985 with Execu Search. Kevin convinced me to give him an opportunity when he stated I would not regret hiring him. The decision to hire Kevin turned out to be a very sound business decision and certainly an advantage for Execu Search. He was instrumental in opening our first branch office in Atlanta. It turned out to be one of the most successful offices in the entire organization. What I most remember about Kevin was his consistency in demonstrating his Christian values and how he implemented his belief in Christ into the Executive recruiting industry. I see nothing but greatness in Kevin, and he will be successful in any arena in of life. I am honored to call him my friend."

Chapter Take-Aways

Please write down several points you want to remember and apply from this chapter.

CHAPTER THREE

Prison Ministry/Restoration
Community Resources

Prison Ministry/Restoration Community Resources (RCR)

Dr. Dollar was the visionary of the Prison Ministry at World Changers Church International. I was fortunate to work with Minister Garner in developing the Prison Ministry. Within several years, the prison ministry expanded to partner with 20 institutions: The Federal Penitentiary in Atlanta, Pulaski State Prison, Metro State Prison, Georgia Diagnostic and Classification State Prison, also known as Jackson State Prison., Atlanta Transitional Center, Fulton County Jail, Parchman State Prison in Mississippi, Florida State Prison, and Dominguez State Jail in San Antonio, Texas are some of the institutions. Over the years, we developed very good relationships with wardens, chaplains, correction officers, and the incarcerated individuals.

When an individual returns to prison after being released, this is referred to as recidivism, which is defined as reverting back to criminal behavior and ultimately returning to incarceration. This usually occurs when there is no support system in place for the male or female individual being released.

Now, many of the individuals we ministered to in the institutions were coming to the church to receive assistance with food, shelter, and a support system to help them reenter society.

Restoration Community Resources (RCR)

Restoration Community Resources was founded by Minister Tommie Garner and Brent Williams. The organization was created as a vehicle to assist men in successfully reentering society after incarceration.

I was asked to serve on the Board of Directors by the founders. After a few years in operation, Minister Garner and Brent Williams decided to restructure RCR and asked if I would assume exclusive leadership of the organization as they desired to pursue other ventures. I prayed about the opportunity and accepted. I am thankful and grateful to Minister Garner and Brent Williams for affording me the opportunity to be a part of Restoration Community Resources.

At the time of the restructuring of the organization, the Aftercare Housing Program (Discipleship House), Entrepreneurial Mentoring Program, and the Scholarship Program had not been established.

Aftercare Housing Program: The Discipleship House

The housing component would allow the individuals being released from incarceration a stable and reliable support system. After months of investigating several apartment complexes, I located an apartment complex and met with the management.

The management team was open to the vision of housing ex-offenders and agreed on second-chance pilot program. The complex agreed to rent Restoration Community Resources a three-bedroom apartment as a test to the pilot program.

Six men, who I refer to as the Pillars of the Aftercare Program, dedicated their time to conduct group sessions for the ex-offenders once a week. The group sessions included bible study, financial literacy, the importance of integrity in life, the importance of being responsible and respectful of other people's property, and how to be a positive person.

These pillars were:

Minister Williams Glenn
Minister Danny Gardner
Elder Mark Payne
Darrell Temple
Bernard Lawson
Adam Roby

Because of the group sessions, the ex-offenders were outstanding residents, and the housing component expanded. Within two years, the apartment complex was renting three three-bedroom apartments to RCR.

After the third year at the apartment complex, we qualified to purchase a four-bedroom house. After securing the house, we named it The Discipleship House.

After being involved in the Prison Ministry for two decades, we understood the importance of having a secure support system to keep the ex-offenders accountable and build their confidence as they adjusted back into society.

We understood that after being incarcerated for years, reentering society was going to have challenges. While in prison, many of their decisions were already selected, such as what time to go to bed, what clothes to wear, and what was served for breakfast, lunch, and dinner. Making these types of day-to-day decisions was not common for those being released from incarceration.

The Waffle House was a major supporter of hiring the residents from the Discipleship House.

In addition to the group sessions, we incorporated apprenticeship programs with electricians, painters, and landscapers. Having marketable skills was helpful to be able to enter and succeed in the workplace. Being able to secure gainful employment coming out of prison was a major obstacle that could be discouraging.

I want to say thank you to Can Do Electric Company owner Dewayne Mosley for believing in the apprentice program and being our first apprentice company.

I also want to thank Dr. Dollar and World Changers Church International for their support and encouragement with the Aftercare Program and The Discipleship House.

The Entrepreneurial Mentoring Program

During the transition from the Prison Ministry, the Aftercare Program and the Discipleship House. I was approached by several parents who desired their son's to develop a understanding of Business and Marketing concepts.

In developing the Entrepreneurial Mentoring Program utilizing the entrepreneurial skills acquired from the recruiting industry was essential. The focus core group would be 9 years old to eighteen years old.

Business men Danny Gardner and William Glenn were the foundation of the Entrepreneurial Mentoring Program. We believed we had a unique concept to expose business acumen which would compliment our vision and mission.

Vision
To successfully impact the lives of young men through mentorship with emphasis on education and exposure to entrepreneurial endeavors.

Mission
To assist young men in recognizing and fulfilling their purpose in life.

We would provide **services** in these areas:

- Community Involvement
- "Speaking in Excellence" Seminar
- College Preparation
- Financial Investment Education
- Networking
- Personal and Professional Grooming

After several months, the attendance began to increase as the young entrepreneurs started to invite their friends. We began noticing the gifts being revealed within the young entrepreneurs. They had desires to create business opportunities and to learn how to operate businesses.

The Young Entrepreneurs decided to start a company called " Men of Valor Enterprises (MOVE) the company manufactures Tee Shirts and Hoodies. The company is incorporated in the state of Georgia.

Restoration Community Resources received a Trademark on our motto, “A Window Of Opportunity.” We want the young entrepreneurs to be able to achieve whatever they desire. The trademark “A Window of Opportunity” is a constant reminder to the young entrepreneurs: whatever you are willing to pursue, there is an opportunity for you to accomplish your desires.

Restoration Community Resources has awarded to date 70 scholarships to the Young Entrepreneurs that completed the program and graduated from High School.

We know the youth are our future; we want them to be prepared.

Success Stories about Restoration Community Resources

Elston Montford II

"I have participated in The Restoration Community Resources Entrepreneurial Mentoring program for eight years. This program has been one of the most influential parts of my development in my life. The services provided from the public speaking seminars, financial education, college tours, and the scholarship program assisted me as I completed my Bachelor of Science in Veterinary Technology from Fort Valley State University, in December 2021.
Graduated from Kansas State University with a Masters Degree in Biomedical Science September 2025. I am looking forward to attending Veterinarian School.

The most important foundation of the program to me is the excellent life advice and commitment the mentors give to the young men who are in the program.
I am forever thankful and grateful to the mentors who I know will be a relevant part of my life as long as I live.

I would like to personally thank my Father for putting me in a position to learn from the mentors of Restoration Community Resources.

"I am forever grateful for our mentoring group, because it propelled me in life."

Justyn Seivright

(KPMG employee, one of the Big Four Accounting Firms)

"Restoration Community Resources (RCR) has impacted my life drastically. Since I joined the mentoring group around 8 years ago, it has been beneficial and supportive to my growth. The mentors and young entrepreneurs sacrifice their time to spread wisdom to the youth. As a member of this organization, we worked on things like networking, public speaking, and financial literacy.

RCR has kept me active in the community and outside of home with several events. We participated in events like the 5k run, trip to D.C., and business awards. RCR has been like a second family to me, and I will take it all with me as I progress in life. Additionally, I was awarded a scholarship by Restoration Community Resources to assist in my finances to attend Mount St. Mary's University, where I received my Bachelor of Arts degree in Finance in 2018 and my Master's in the spring of 2023."

Curtis Blount, Jr.
(United State Army Captain)

"People may ask, '*How* did Restoration Community Resources (RCR) help transition you from high school to college?' With great respect and privilege, I would talk to the mentors and receive wonderful advice."

"Personally, the guidance I had within myself was not enough for the transition from high school to college. Minister Kevin Smith blessed me with his words of encouragement, the opportunity to become a leader in the community, and the capacity to acquire my home. The scholarship I received was very helpful towards my college education. The exposure to the business principles and the many business owners in the community was invaluable."

"I had a smooth transition because of the prestigious entrepreneur mentoring program. With great humility, I will always be honored to be a part of our group as a mentor to give back what I have learned and experienced. During several group discussions, we may elaborate on treating yourself with great character outside of your home. One thing I have learned is to keep your morals and values in perspective. When individuals have those two characteristics, I know that, the transition from high school to college will be smoother and less stressful."

Justin Payne
(Author of I AM NOT MY PAST)

"The year was 2007 when I became part of Discipleship House in College Park, Georgia. I had already witnessed my father die in prison from cancer. I knew the sacrifice would be worth it. The discipleship was occupied by grown men, recovering addicts, and individuals making a transition from prison back into society. I was the youngest person in the house when I was 17. What I experienced in the discipleship house was a sense of peace."

"Before that, I was in prison for a number of years and needed direction. The discipleship house did not need me; I needed the program that they provided. I would like to say thank you, Minister Kevin Smith, for planting a seed of hope in a young man coming from a hopeless place. I served my time in prison, and the seed of hope is now a tree of life spreading knowledge and wisdom into young men and women. Today I write to you as a college graduate with multiple degrees who teaches welding techniques in multiple institutions in the State of Georgia."

Desmond Jackson

"In March of 2013, I, along with five other classmates, started a clothing line named Avant Society. However, my passion and knowledge of entrepreneurship did not begin in 2013. It actually started many years prior and has been polished for more than eight years by the Restoration Community Resources Entrepreneurial Mentoring Group. During my participation in the program, I not only developed my business acumen, but learned valuable lessons that have helped me as a businessman and as a person. I learned how to speak in public, tie a tie, work with others, develop a business plan, and a plethora of other skills and traits that I picked up from the talented and exceptionally wise mentors who were placed before me.

If it were not for the RCR Entrepreneurial Mentoring Group, I would not have the current passion for success and business, as well as the pride to want to work for myself instead of working for others. I received a scholarship from the Restoration Community Resources Entrepreneur Mentoring Program to assist with my financial obligations as I attended Valdosta University and received a Bachelor of Arts in Marketing."

Ashton Soles

"Growing up, my father was an accountant, and my mother worked in the airline industry. We were not wealthy, but my parents made sure my sisters and I had everything we needed. They laid a strong foundation for us at home, even though the world outside was shifting. Metro Atlanta was dealing with rising crime, limited resources, and changing schools. It often felt like the community was being pulled in different directions. In that environment, choices were always present. The right and wrong paths were clear, but navigating them was not always straightforward.

As I look back, I realize how much the people around me shaped my life. The friendships that I formed, the mentors who guided me, and the organizations I became part of played a significant role in helping navigate those challenging times.

One group in particular stands out: **Restoration Community Resources (RCR)**.

I first encountered RCR when I started high school. At that point, I was already exploring entrepreneurship and doing well academically, but I was still figuring out who I wanted to be.

RCR became a game-changer. It introduced me to successful professionals who had built their careers through hard work while staying grounded in their faith. They were more than just mentors, ; they were role models, showing me what was possible with focus and dedication. They held me accountable, encouraged me, and provided a safe space to explore my ideas.

RCR did not just teach me about business, ; it showed me what it means to live with integrity. I learned valuable skills such as public speaking, financial management, networking, and how to start a business. The scholarship I received from RCR assisted me as I attended Florida A&M, where I received a Bachelor of Science in Business Administration.

However, what I gained from RCR went beyond professional skills. The sense of brotherhood I found there is invaluable. It shaped me as a leader, a quality that followed me when I joined the Beta Nu Chapter of Alpha Phi Alpha Fraternity, Inc. But more than anything, the spiritual guidance I received had the deepest impact. The Christian values woven into the program strengthened my relationship with God, and that connection has been my guiding force ever since.

Looking back, I can see how instrumental RCR was in helping me become the person I am today. That is why I am so passionate about giving back. I am committed to guiding the next generation of young men, helping them discover their potential just as RCR helped me unlock mine. Becoming a mentor with RCR has afforded me the opportunity to contribute to an organization that is rooted in preparing leaders, a place where young men can grow into leaders who strive for something greater than themselves. This is the legacy I hope to pass on."

Jarod A. Anderson

"The Impact of Restoration Community Resources on My Life: It's almost hard to put into words the immense impact Restoration Community Resources has had on my life and that of my family. As with most of the young entrepreneurs who go through the program, it was never my desire to participate in the program. I was doing a favor by accompanying a young lad to the program, whom I had been mentoring through another family-based mentoring program. Little did I know that God was using these circumstances to create a divine connection that would change my life's trajectory forever. All I did was continue to show up, often grudgingly. Unbeknownst to me, over the years, I was developing into more of a man just like the boys we were mentoring.

It's been almost twenty years since those early days, and I can confidently say that the mentoring program is blessing me more today than ever. Being in the presence of the men in the program gave me a model of manhood and fatherhood that I would not have received from my father alone. Although a mentor, I have always received mentoring from Minister Kevin and other men in the program in profound and often imperceptible ways. Through my relationship with Kevin, I was being prepped and prepared to become the husband, father, and Man of God I am today. He has been there for me in the best and the worst of times.

To say my time in the mentoring program has been fulfilling and rewarding would be an understatement. I have received so much more in proportion to what I have given.

Recently, I have had the immense privilege of bringing my son to the mentoring program at eight years old. To sit next to him while he receives the same mentorship that helped frame me into the father I am to him is simply an amazing feeling. I am so excited to see where he will be after ten years in the program.

Needless to say, I will be forever grateful to Minister Kevin and the Restoration Community Resources Mentoring Program for all they have done for me and my family."

Chapter Take-Aways

Please write down several points you want to remember and apply from this chapter.

CHAPTER FOUR

Success and Convenience Cannot Exist Together

When you are exiting your comfort zone to pursue your goals and aspirations, it is inevitable that you will be growing and changing. As you grow and change, it is totally natural to feel uncomfortable. When you are in the phase two stage (the process and actions), you will be growing and stretching yourself because you are out of your area of comfort.

Convenience

It is unusual to reach your level of success and experience convenience at the same time. Success and convenience do not exist at the same space.

When you are on your journey to success, it is unusual to have comfort and convenience at the same time. The road to success is not void of obstacles, and sometimes the road to success includes failure.

Success and Convenience do not go together on your journey. Quick example: Oil and water in a jar will eventually separate.

We all have choices. Dreams do not just happen; Dreams requires plan of action.

Success and convenience do not go together.

I learned to gain encouragement from my failures. If I had not experienced disappointment, I would not have appreciated the hard work needed to accomplish my goals. The journey really is as important as the destination.

What I learned from my experiences is that the road to accomplishing my goals was bumpy and inconvenient. This is not discouragement, but reality.

I needed to maintain a mind-set of moving forward. I believed I would overcome the obstacles I faced.

When we limit ourselves to comfortable activities, we will get the same old results. Being comfortable with where you are now will not help you reach your goals. To achieve new and different results, we need to make adjustments in our everyday life activities. In short, we must follow through with our plan of action.

Here's an example of some choices we make while on our journey. As you read the example, you may realize you have similar choices to make.

The example is about Jim, but it could be anyone. Jim wanted to complete a specialized computer science class, and he thought it was a high priority for him. The class was offered once a year on Tuesday evenings from 7pm to 9pm. His two favorite television shows were also shown on Tuesday evenings from 7pm to 9pm.

He needed to make a decision.

He could choose comfort and convenience (continue watching the television shows) and take the class at another time. Or he could record the show and watch them in the future.

When you approach your life and decisions with integrity, you will stick to your plan of action so that you can accomplish your goal.

Jim reviewed his options with a sense of integrity. He went into a decision-making process.

- **Why? What's In It For Me? (WIIFM):-** Completing the computer class will equip me with the required skills for a substantial salary increase and job promotion.
- **Fact:** The class will require several hours of studying per week for 14 weeks, plus time in the class.
- **Results and Value:** Are the potential results valuable enough for me to make the necessary adjustments to my schedule?

When I shared this example during one of our mentoring sessions, many young men responded that the person should take the class. Many students thought the decision was a "no-brainer" because there would be a substantial increase in Jim's income and a promotion at the same time! Are you willing to make sacrifices to achieve your goals?

I share this story because it is a valuable example of making sacrifices to achieve our goals.

- What in your personal life are you willing to rearrange so that you complete a task or goal?

____

____

____

____

Success requires you to exit your comfort zone and rearrange your priorities.

Whether you prefer success or convenience is totally up to you. The perfect time will NOT come.

We need to recognize that we can invest in our lives by making a written plan of action and then following up to implement the plan. We put in effort and apply as much perseverance and knowledge as possible.

> Integrity and character involve carrying out our plans of action to achieve our desired results. Remember, challenges are part of the journey.

Success does not come to people because they desire it. You can have excuses or results, but you cannot have both.

We all have choices. For example, you can be a dreamer and take little action. Or you can be a dreamer who follows through in getting to your destination.

Be careful who you listen to.

The decisions we make to accomplish our goals may not be well-received by our friends or family members. That is their opinion. Their opinion does not make your goals unworthy or unattainable. What can make your goals unattainable is your desire to please everyone along the way.

Avoid making excuses. Make results.

I encourage you to move past challenges and continue to make accomplishments on your journey to your destination. Ask for help when needed.

Do you know people who have "great intentions," but they don't move forward?

Many goals remain intentions instead of accomplishments because the person does not execute their plan of action.

To be successful, integrity will be a part of the process. Remember, integrity is a purposeful quality. We follow through and take action.

Character development includes taking action and having integrity.

Take action.

Whether we desire to lose weight, increase our exercise, or pursue a new career, we need to take action. It is important that we do not remain in a state of intention.

Make your decision. Create a plan. Follow through with your plan.

Intention	Decision/Action
I intend to exercise more.	• I decide to exercise more. • I join a specific gym. • I set my schedule for daily exercise. • I go to the gym and exercise.
I intend to eat healthier.	• I decide to eat healthy foods. • I determine the healthy foods to eat. • I eat healthy foods
I intend to be a more positive person.	• I choose to have a positive attitude. • I take time to appreciate my life.
I intend to be successful in my new job.	• I decide to learn as much as possible about my job. • I decide to be teachable and coachable in my new position. • I apply what I learn to help me be successful

**Make your decision. Do not live with "good intentions."
Follow through with an action plan.**

I decided to play football for Trenton Central High School.

The year I decided to play football, I failed the physical because of a breathing problem. It was challenging to watch the game from the bleachers as a fan and not being on the field with the team. The team did great and went undefeated. Some of the players went onto Division I colleges. For me, it was a time of learning to overcome obstacles and disappointments.

My breathing problem went away. During the summer before my next year, I put together a plan of action.

I established a workout routine that would prepare me for the upcoming football tryouts. I ran every morning and early evening, lifted weights, and practiced running various passing routes. I wanted to play receiver. It was my goal to play on the field, not sit on the bench.

In the fall, tryouts for the football team began. I remember the first day as being humbling to me. The returning players received their equipment first. The rest of us received whatever was left. I remained positive, although every piece of equipment was too big for me. I got my equipment. It was time for the tryouts to begin. Being an unknown person on the team, I had to prove myself on every play. The best part of tryouts was that they were conducted in the mornings and in the afternoons. I had two chances to make a positive impression on the coaches.

I impressed the coaches enough to play on the practice squad. This was the squad that the starting offensive and defensive teams played against to prepare for upcoming games. We had scrimmages for approximately six weeks before the actual season started.

Then I got a surprise.

My dad sat me down after practice one night and asked me, *"How is practice coming along?"* My response was, *"Great."* Dad said, *"Good, because if you're not a consistent player, I will need you to work in the garden."* In all fairness, my dad gave me one of my first lessons about being a consistent person.

Thank you, Dad.

I had a clear choice in front of me: Be a consistent player or work in the garden after school and attend the games as a fan.

My dad's comments increased my desire to be on the team. During the remaining time on the practice squad, I had one goal, and that was to be a consistent player. My attitude was "I was going to have to earn my place on the team." Whatever it took to be impressive on the field, I would do it.

Looking back later in life, I realized it was an important lesson for me. Thank you, Dad. Because I had a clear objective, I did not stop or get sidetracked before I got to my destination.

Ask yourself, are you operating from "good intentions," or have you made a decision to reach your destination?

The good news is that I was successful in securing a position on the high school football team during my junior year. I was also able to dedicate time to the household chores, so everyone was a winner. During my senior year, I became a starter on offense (as a receiver) and on defense (as an outside linebacker).

Be prepared when the opportunity presents itself.

> *"The supreme quality for leadership*
> *is unquestionably integrity.*
> *Without it, no real success is possible,*
> *no matter whether it is*
> *on a section gang, on a football field,*
> *in an army, or in an office."*
>
> ~Dwight D. Eisenhower

Chapter Take-Aways

Please write down several points you want to remember and apply from this chapter.

CHAPTER FIVE

Preparation and Execution: Do Not Run Another Person's Race

Do not compare yourself to others.

As I was playing sports in high school, the lesson that became a standard for me in life was **"do not compare myself with others."**

Preparation and Execution.

During my high school senior year, I was able to experience the preparation and execution that I teach today.

After football season, I was a member of a very successful track team. We were preparing for the city championship track and field meet. If you were a track runner, you wanted to compete in this track event because it was one of the biggest sports events of the year.

To qualify for this meet, you had to be a top performer in the city. My event was the 800 meters.

Because it was such an important and perhaps life-changing event in my life, I took the liberty of inviting several family members and friends to attend. Race day was perfect; not too hot. It was a great day for an outdoor spring track meet.

It was high stakes; the college scouts and newspaper reporters would be attending.

The coach and my teammates were depending on me to place in the top three positions. I felt ready because I knew I had prepared myself with strong and consistent training for this day.

Yikes. I finished in sixth place, certainly not in the top three. I was incredibly disappointed and embarrassed by my performance.

I have never forgotten what took place after the race. My track coach came over to me, and before he opened his mouth, I asked, *"Coach, what just happened?"*

He gently put his arm around me and whispered in my ear, *"I know exactly what just happened."* As my coach smiled at me, I was anxiously waiting to hear more about why I lost such an important race in the presence of family members, friends, teammates, classmates, college recruiters, and the newspaper reporters.

Smith is the name he called me, and he said, *"Smith, you have the heart of a champion, and you trained like a champion who expected to win this race. I personally trained you to win this race."* He continued, *"You decided to disregard your training. You stopped trusting in your preparation. You decided to run another man's race."*

Coach continued. *"The competition started out fast, and you got behind. Instead of doing what you trained to do, you decided to run to the front of the runners. Our plan was for you to stay in the middle of the runners and, only in the second lap, take the lead."*

We began talking about the race that I ran. By staying in the lead for most of the race, it appeared as if everything was working out well, even though this was not what the coach and I had prepared for.

When it was my time to dig deep inside myself for the final 200 meters, I was exhausted, and I felt like I was wearing lead shoes. I was unable to finish strong.

That very day in my senior year in high school, I learned a valuable lesson.

We can be inspired by other people, and we can learn from them, but we do not want to compare ourselves to them. Encourage yourself and be prepared for the opportunity you want to take.

You can never run another person's race and expect to win. You must run the race in life that you have prepared yourself to win.

When you trust your preparation and execution, you are displaying your integrity.

I remember that during the early years of my executive recruiting career, I would attend meetings with Vice Presidents and Regional Directors who were decision-makers for their companies. I had to be confident in trusting my preparation, execution, and stay focused on accomplishing my task.

For example, when I was contracted by the pharmaceutical company to assist in hiring a national sales force, this was a time for me to run my own race. It was a major contract with salespeople being hired throughout the country. Prior to the sales representatives being hired, there was a meeting with the company's Executive Sales team and Regional and Division Managers from the four regions of the country. - I represented Execu Search.

If I had not been prepared to encounter a meeting of this magnitude; , I would have been intimidated and nervous. The main concern of most of the sales managers was whether or not Execu Search had the ability to recruit at this level.

There were suggestions made to the Human Resources Director that this assignment may be more than Execu Search could handle. I reassured the Human Resources Director that they had made the right decision to hire our firm, and the assignment would be completed on time. I was confident when I told the Director they would be pleased with the results.

I did not allow the atmosphere and the negative comments from the top management to stop me from moving forward with the contract. There was tremendous pressure to perform.

I was confident in our experience and preparation to complete this contract. The assignment was very challenging and required teamwork and integrity from everyone involved in the project.

Everyone had to perform with excellence, and there was no room for excuses. The contract was completed on time, and the company gave Execu Search an outstanding rating.

Lesson learned: You can accomplish the goal when you are properly prepared. When you are properly prepared, you do not have to compare yourself to others.

The same can be true about taking an exam. You prepare yourself, and you will be ready. But then before the exam, you hear how someone else has prepared. Do you rethink your strategy at the last minute, or do you stay with your preparation? Make sure you run your own race.

Remember, you cannot doubt your preparation-; it will hinder you from reaching your goal.

When you have a sincere desire to complete your goals, here are some of the actions that you must implement:

- **Preparation**
- **Be Disciplined**
- **Execution of your plan of action**

Chapter Take-Aways

Please write down several points you want to remember and apply from this chapter.

CHAPTER SIX

Test of Commitment: Why Integrity Matters

Commitments matter when meeting with people.

When we tell another person we are going to meet them at the mall at 3 pm, and we show up at 3 pm, this shows our commitment and integrity to the other person. The same is true if we say we will help with the household chores and we follow up with our actions to do what we said we would do. Similarly, if we say we are going to do something for a co-worker, we are demonstrating our integrity and character to that person when we follow up with what we said we would do. It's the same when you are on a team. Congratulations to you for your following through.

Do you make commitments to yourself?

When you set a goal of making more money and you develop a plan to do that, and you work on your plan, that is demonstrating commitment and integrity to yourself. Congratulations to you.

When you make a commitment to someone and do not follow through on your commitment, that demonstrates something about you.

When I say I am going to show up at 3 pm and I don't show up until 4 pm for the get-together without notifying that person that I will be late, what am I demonstrating about my character and integrity?

When I "forget" to complete the chores that I have agreed to do, what am I demonstrating about my character and integrity?

Whether we follow up on our word, or not, we are developing habits. With our habits, it is very important to ask ourselves, *"Are the habits helping me, or are they limiting me?"*

Commitment is an agreement or pledge to do something in the future.

Would you be willing to give your time and energy to something or someone you believe in? If you truly commit yourself to something or someone, the actions you take will speak louder than your words.

- What is the purpose of your commitment?
- When you look at commitment, will your actions correspond to the words you have spoken?

Commitment will be tested before the completion of the goal.

The Phil Crescenzo Story – Commitment Exemplified

What I am about to share is a true example of commitment exemplified.

This is a true story about Phil Crescenzo, his two sons, his brother Dave, and many team members. Phil and his brother had a thriving family business. Due to the economic collapse in 2008, they saw business revenues substantially decrease.

To help their business, they decided to attend a company convention to gain knowledge that would enhance their supplemental business. During the convention, they asked each other the following questions:

- Why did we attend the convention?
- What goals do we hope to accomplish?
- What could stop us from reaching our goals?
- What is our action plan to reach our goals?

During the convention, they were creating action plans and making commitments to ensure there was a clear direction so that they would achieve their goals.

Heading back to New Jersey from the convention, Phil and his wife were notified that there was a tragic accident involving two of their oldest grandchildren. They were informed they were both killed instantly.

The loss was paralyzing, but the support was greater. Phil conducted the funeral service as hundreds came to pay their respects. The love and support were overwhelming.

What would happen to Phil and his wife, their family members, and their team?

Anyone would certainly understand if commitments that had been established at the convention were delayed or forgotten.

Instead, Phil decided to follow through with the commitments made to his family and team members. Phil and the team's decision to move forward with their commitments changed the trajectory of not only the Crescenzo family but tens of thousands of their peers for over a decade.

Additionally, Phil and his wife have now been able to invest in other business ventures, including a famous country club in Georgetown, South Carolina.

Chapter Take-Aways

Please write down several points you want to remember and apply from this chapter.

CHAPTER SEVEN

Consistency Always Brings Results

Practicing Consistency and Integrity

The patterns we practice every day develop into habits that represent us as individuals.

Do you know anyone who is always late for an event? The person is always late, no matter what the occasion. When a person has a habit of "always being late," that action influences how other people view them.

Being Consistent Helped Me Seize an Opportunity.

Some time ago, at a restaurant, I noticed several men in the restaurant had their ties laid over their shoulders. This technique is designed to protect their ties while they eat.

However, this technique has been known to fail, which means the tie can get food or drink on it. Getting a tie professionally cleaned can be costly. As I continued to observe all these men with their ties over their shoulders, an idea came to me. *"What if I could come up with a device that could protect their ties?"*

I did a little market research right in the restaurant. I left my table and asked several gentlemen in the restaurant this question: *"If I could provide something that could protect your tie while you were eating, would you wear it?"*.
Their enthusiastic response was *"Absolutely!"*

This would be a great invention! Based on my experience, I did not think a tie protector had been invented, at least I had never seen one. I did research at the patent section of the library to determine if a tie protector patent already existed. - That proved to be good news because there was no patent for a tie protector. The thought of me becoming an inventor was exciting, and pursuing this possibility would be challenging. And I like challenges.

As I shared with some friends and family about my project, some responses were positive and encouraging. Yet, other comments were negative or lukewarm at best.

My point is this: Everyone may not see your own vision the same way you do.

Everyone is entitled to their opinion, but I could not allow other people's opinions to affect my efforts. I heard lots of questions such as. *"How do you know the concept will work?" "Who are you going to market the product to?" "How much will it cost you to bring it to the market?" "How will you distribute the product?"* - I knew these were legitimate and important questions.
My response was: *"I don't have all the answers at this point. But I'm going to pursue the idea one step at a time."*

We need to stay at it, even when we do not have all the answers. This is where my resourcefulness took over. I visited the patent library, which gave me insight on how to effectively write the description of the tie protector product.

To be successful, I needed to be consistent.

My tie protector invention was completely out of my comfort zone. This was certainly a journey full of life lessons and integrity investments. There is a process of getting a product into the market. There are monetary investments made during this process. I knew nothing about developing a product or prototype; I had to find a qualified individual to walk me through the process.

I was referred to Antonio Anderson, who had been successful in going through the patent process; in fact, his invention was in the marketplace and doing well.

Antonio assisted me in putting together a prototype. The prototype looked like what I had imagined, but it did not perform as I expected. We put together a focus group of individuals to eat dinner, try the tie protector, and give us feedback on the product. We received valuable feedback that made us realize that we had to redesign the product for it to be effective, and also be attractive to the buyer. The focus group also allowed us to determine a price that would be competitive. Antonio assisted me in finding a manufacturer, and because the product had to be redesigned, we had to apply for an additional patent to protect our investment.

When situations come up while we are pursuing a goal, we can get discouraged. On the other hand, we can choose to see the situation as an opportunity to make adjustments along the journey. I encourage you to remain focused on the destination.

Being consistent at this point was critical because discouragement and negative thoughts can affect your decision-making. Have positive expectations.
And remember that everyone may not provide encouragement to your projects and goals.

I received the patent and trademark. I received the shipment of **Smithi Tie Protectors.**

The introduction/reception event was successful. The mentoring group participated in the product launch, which was a great experience for the young entrepreneurs, to witness the Tie Protector from a concept to the final product. It was a life lesson of "A Window of Opportunity," regardless of one's age.

Perseverance was the key. The Smithi Tie Protector invention appeared on the first episode of the first season of a game TV show called Snake Oil.
This opportunity wouldn't have presented itself without consistency.

Remember, consistency and integrity are linked together.

People may hear what you say, but they believe what you do. Which means, your actions should match your words. Your words and actions become how people describe you.

Chapter Take-Aways

Please write down several points you want to remember and apply from this chapter.

CHAPTER EIGHT

"I will try" is not enough;
you need a plan of action.

A plan of action is a written document that provides guidance for completing your journey. The more you use a written plan of action, the more you will appreciate its power to help you maintain being committed and focused. You can use a plan of action for any goal you want to achieve.

What are some of the elements in a plan of action?

An action plan helps people on their journey.

These questions can help you:

- Why do you want to achieve the goal?
- What actions are required by me to achieve the goal?
- What can I do to evaluate my progress?
- When do you want to complete this goal?

Remember, setbacks on your journey are temporary.

Even with a plan of action, you may experience delays and disappointments, which I refer to as *"temporary setbacks."* I encourage you to have a mind-set that setbacks are temporary. You may want to go back and review Chapter One, which discussed Start, Stop, Continue, and Finish.

No one is exempt from failure. You are the one who needs to decide not to allow temporary setbacks to stop you from accomplishing your goal. Remember, you can use challenges as encouragement during your journey to your destination. When you reach your destination, you will recognize the importance of the challenges that you allowed to encourage you during your journey.

When you operate from *"good intentions,"* you are not committed to finishing. I ask that you develop a plan for completing your goal(s). Remember, integrity is what keeps us focused and helps us finish what we have started.

Are you committed to your goal?

Have you ever asked a person to do something, and they replied, *"I will try."*

Would you agree that the response is not very convincing? Have you ever heard anyone say, *"I'm going to try to lose some weight!"?* Do you think the person is committed to losing weight?

"Try" is not a word of completion.

You may intend to finish a college degree. The degree is 75% complete; you intend to complete the degree in a year. Will you complete the degree, or will it remain an intention? Do you have a plan of action, and are you committed to finishing the work to earn your degree?

If you continue to operate in intentions, you will remain the same.

Do you want to avoid procrastination? Do not intend. Make a commitment

Do you want to be known for your intentions or your completions?

Intentions will not complete the task.

The choice is yours to make.

Every day, your intentions to complete something are challenged. However, the choice is up to you:

- Do you finish with integrity? or
- Do you operate only with intentions?

We should not allow our aspirations and dreams to remain as mere intentions; we need to follow through to accomplish our goals.

Intentions can cause your words not to be valued, because intention is not the same as completion.

Be a person that has a plan of action with a completion date.

Finishing is important because it means you have gone from words to actions. **What matters is that you finish what you start.**

Starting is important, and we need to applaud that. If we do not start, we cannot approach the finish.

Finishing.

Finishing is what we accomplish when we decide to focus on and follow through with our plan of action. When we operate with integrity, we stay on the course and finish without excuses.

Overcome your distractions so that you finish.

Distractions can cause us to remain in intentions.

What distractions do you have in your life that pull you away from integrity?

Are you carefully managing your time so that you remain focused on your vision and action plan?

Finishing demonstrates that goals and desires can be completed. Intentions may give us hope for a short time, but in the end, hope is deferred because the intention does not have a completion date. Be committed to your dreams and stay committed to what you believe you can accomplish.

Finishing is a vital part of life. **In writing this book, the greatest message is to be a finisher. It takes focused effort to finish.**

When we fail to plan, we plan to fail.

A plan of completion is as important as a plan to start. You need a plan to finish. When discouragement, disappointment, or distraction happens, you must have a plan in place to stay focused on the finish line. Without a plan, you can revert back to what is comfortable. As we create our plan of action, we must see ourselves successfully completing our goal more than we see ourselves quitting or not finishing.

Integrity is the anchor that will keep you focused on the commitment you established.

We cannot follow a plan that does not exist.

Stay at it.

I have a friend who is currently a Certified Public Accountant (CPA). It took them several attempts to pass the exam. They remained focused and passed the exam. They completed their goal. On their Certified Public Accountant License, it doesn't read that it took them several attempts to successfully pass the exam. It states that they are a Certified Public Accountant.

What matters is your focus on completing the goal.

Allow your consistency and persistence to overcome challenges and disappointments. Give yourself encouragement because you got yourself back on track to move forward, so that you can complete your goal or dream without excuses.

I believe in you!

It is your time. Go for it!

Be a person of integrity that finishes ... because INTEGRITY FINISHES.

Chapter Take-Aways

Please write down several points you want to remember and apply from this chapter.

Appendix One

Personal Reflective and Group Discussion Questions

- Do you believe integrity is important?

- Why do you believe integrity is important?

- Do you believe you can be successful without integrity?

- How can integrity make an impression in business, in life relationships, in the community, in school?

- How does integrity affect your decisions?

- How can you develop integrity in your life?

Appendix Two

Discussion Questions for Teachers, Parents, Mentors, and Leaders

This appendix provides discussion questions for each chapter that you can use to involve and engage your audience – students, children, employees, volunteers, and so forth. Blank lines are provided for your additional questions.

Chapter One – Your Journey is Just as Important as the Destination

- How does integrity fit into finishing a project? (What does that mean to you?)
- Why is integrity important when developing a plan of action?
- What should I think about when I want to quit?
- How do I remain focused when I encounter an unexpected journey?

___

___

___

Chapter Two – Integrity Challenges and Investments

- What is more important to you, speaking about integrity or being an example of Integrity?

- When you do not honor your commitment, does that decision affect others?

- How would you describe how the testimonials impacted you?

- What integrity investments are you making?

____

____

____

Chapter Three – Prison Ministry/Restoration Community Resources

- Do you think the aftercare program was helpful to the ex-offenders?
- What are your thoughts on the apartment management team allowing Restoration Community Resources to rent apartments for the ex-offenders second chance pilot program?
- How would you describe how the success stories impacted you?
- Which success story did you enjoy?

____

____

____

Chapter Four – Success and Convenience Cannot Exist Together

- How do you interpret this phrase: "Success and Convenience do not go together."
- What are examples that you've observed where people choose convenience over success?
- What are examples of growing and changing when you choose to pursue a new goal?
- Do you allow the opinions of people to stop you from accomplishing your goals?

____

____

____

Chapter Five – Preparation and Execution: Do Not Run Another Person's Race

- What does "do not compare myself to others" mean to you?
- What's the difference between "preparation" and "execution"?
- What is most important to you, preparation or execution?
- What does "do not run another person's race" mean to you?

____

____

____

Chapter Six – Test of Commitment: Why Integrity Matters

- Do you think commitments are valuable? If so, why?
- How do you recommit yourself to a goal once you have stopped?
- Why is it important to follow through?
- What are examples of people who follow through and people who do not follow through?

____

____

____

Chapter Seven – Consistency Always Brings Results

- When you make a decision not to be consistent, does that decision impact your results?
- When you decide not to be consistent, how do you think it will impact others?
- What keeps you striving toward your idea or vision when people around you imply you should stop?
- Why is it important to be consistent for your own goal achievement?

____

____

____

Chapter Eight – "I will try" is not enough; you need a plan of action

- Is the statement "I will try" a confident response to another person? (Why or why not?)

- Would you trust a person to complete a project if the response to you was "I will try?"

- When you write a plan of action, what elements do you include?

- What does the term "temporary setbacks" mean to you?

____

____

____

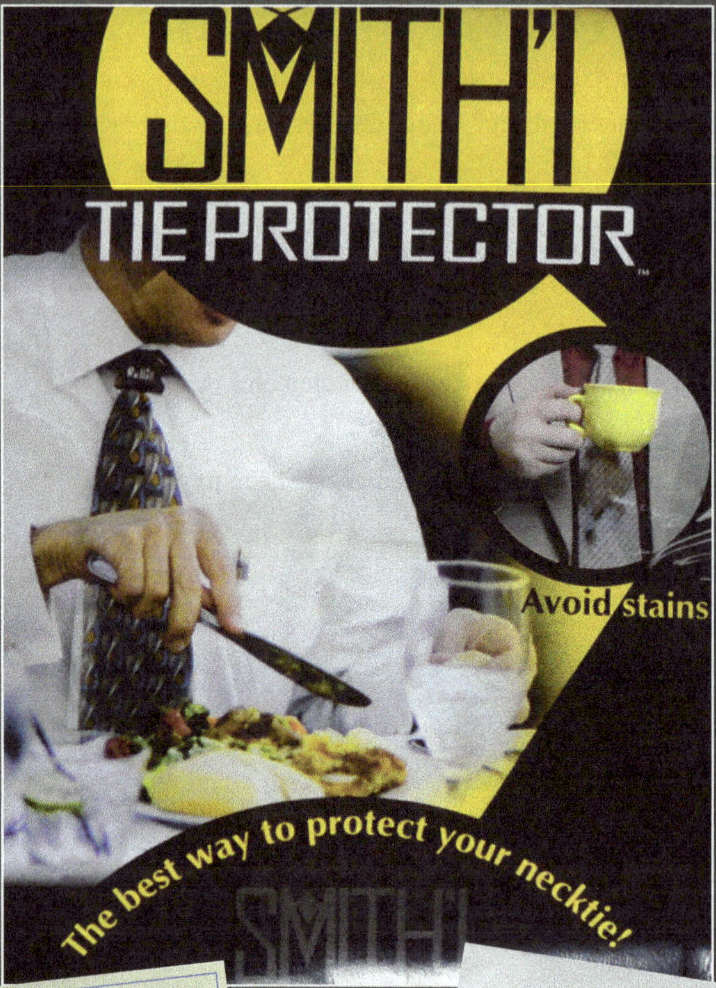

SMITH'I

TIE PROTECTOR™

Avoid stains

The best way to protect your necktie!

SMITH'I

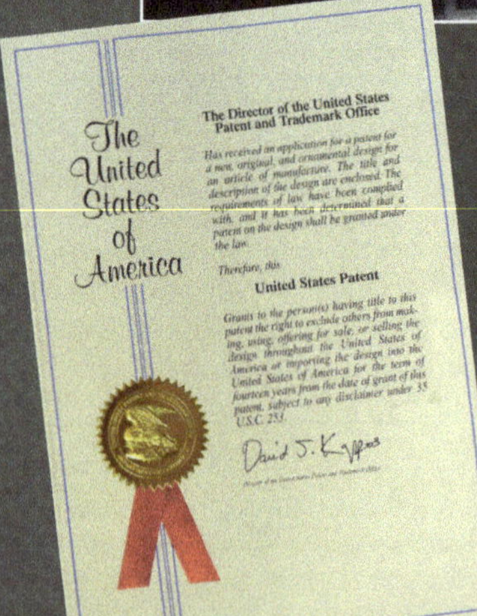

The United States of America

The Director of the United States Patent and Trademark Office

Has received an application for a patent for a new, original, and ornamental design for an article of manufacture. The title and description of the design are enclosed. The requirements of law have been complied with, and it has been determined that a patent on the design shall be granted under the law.

Therefore, this

United States Patent

Grants to the person(s) having title to this patent the right to exclude others from making, using, offering for sale, or selling the design throughout the United States of America or importing the design into the United States of America for the term of fourteen years from the date of grant of this patent, subject to any disclaimer under 35 U.S.C. 253.

David J. Kappos

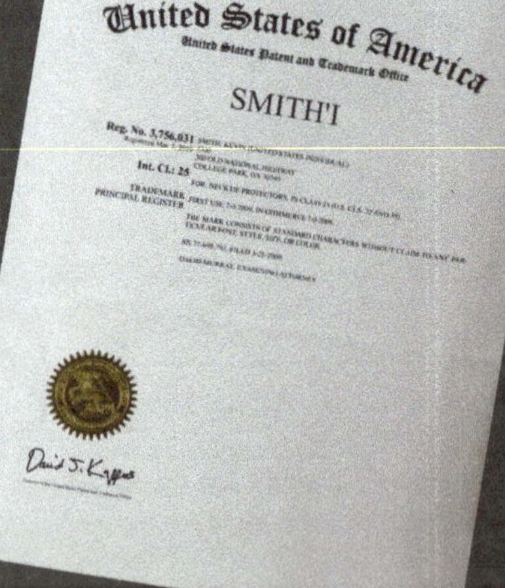

United States of America

United States Patent and Trademark Office

SMITH'I

Reg. No. 3,756,031

Int. Cl.: 25

TRADEMARK
PRINCIPAL REGISTER

THE MARK CONSISTS OF STANDARD CHARACTERS WITHOUT CLAIM TO ANY PARTICULAR FONT, STYLE, SIZE, OR COLOR.

David J. Kappos

www.ingramcontent.com/pod-product-compliance
Lightning Source LLC
LaVergne TN
LVHW010034160826
845671LV00004B/188

* 9 7 8 1 9 5 6 8 8 4 4 0 1 *